EARLY AMERICAN CRAFTS

Tools, Shops and Products

by C. B. COLBY

Coward, McCann & Geoghegan   New York

Contents

Photo Credits

Mystic Seaport, Mystic, Connecticut: Pages 41, 42, 43, 44, 45, 46, 47, 48. Old Sturbridge Village, Sturbridge, Massachusetts: pages 8, 9, 37, upper left. All other photos courtesy of Colonial Williamsburg, Williamsburg, Virginia. Full color cover transparency also courtesy Colonial Williamsburg.

08 up

Library of Congress Catalog Card Number: 67-24212

Fifth Impression
SBN: GB 698-30066-1

Early Crafts and Craftsmen

In the days before power tools, high-speed machinery and production lines, everything was handmade by craftsmen of many skills. Native ingenuity, imagination, and training, plus honest workmanship and pride in their product, enabled these craftsmen to turn out beautiful and functional articles for common use as well as truly artistic masterpieces.

From simple shingles, wooden garden rakes, and candles, to fine jewelry and exquisite furniture, the products of early American craftsmen are much sought after today as priceless examples of beautiful and careful workmanship.

At many historical restorations, you can see the skills of these craftsmen demonstrated. Using the same tools the original craftsmen used, skilled workers turn out duplicates of the early products so that you can see just how they were made.

There were bootmakers, harnessmakers, jewelers, wigmakers, cabinetmakers, clockmakers and many more, including the all-important gunsmith. Each worker spent long months (sometimes years) learning his craft before becoming what was known as a "master craftsman."

Whether a master blacksmith or a master watchmaker, the title was respected and admired by all.

In those days even the tools with which these craftsmen worked their magic in wood, leather and metal often had to be designed and made by the craftsmen themselves, improvising as they needed a new one. Many a simple tool for a specific task designed by some backwoods craftsman remains unimproved upon to this day.

Today, however, these tools can be operated mechanically at higher speeds, a speed which has also eliminated the personal pride of craftsmanship so evident in the patiently handmade products of long ago, whether a simple garden rake or a fine piece of silver or furniture.

Many craftsmen worked with the most common of local woods or iron, the basest of metals, but their products reflected the same pride of workmanship as did those of craftsmen who worked in gold or silver or the rarest of woods from abroad. Almost anything made by their hands is a thing of beauty and lasting pride to today's lucky owners.

As so many of the pioneers and settlers lived far away from centers of manufacturing and trade, a majority of them were skilled in at least one or more essential crafts as a simple matter of survival.

The women could spin and weave, knit and sew, make candles and work in leather. Many could make baskets and fashion shoes as well.

The men could fashion tools and build cabins, houses and rough furniture from trees they felled themselves. They could repair firearms in an emergency, make powder and cast shot, build wagons and repair them. They could use a forge and anvil with sufficient skill to keep their tools sharp, their homes in repair and their firearms ready at all times to defend themselves.

Even the youngsters were craftsmen of a sort, for they gathered the materials for their parents, dipped candles, split shingles and helped with the housework when required, even the spinning and weaving. In those days there were few idle hands of any age, for everyone had to "earn his salt" in one way or another. Not only did the early settlers have to, of necessity, know how to make things, but they took pride in knowing these skills. *Not* to be able to use their hands in both simple and skilled crafts was unthinkable.

On the following pages you will see craftsmen at work and learn about their skills as they are still demonstrated at some of America's most popular and famous historical restorations. Many are shown in costumes typical of the periods in which their crafts flourished so briskly. When you visit such restorations, I am sure you will find a new appreciation for what our ancestors could do with simple tools and skillful hands. I hope this book will encourage you to visit any such restoration near you, and perhaps develop a desire to learn, yourselves, how to practice some of these fine arts.

I must express my sincere appreciation to all those who helped me with this book and provided the outstanding photographs, especially such fine folks as Mr. James J. Keeney, Director of the News Bureau of Old Sturbridge Village, Sturbridge, Massachusetts, and Mrs. Alma Eshenfelder, Publicity Director of Mystic Seaport, Mystic, Connecticut. In particular I would like to give my warmest thanks to Mr. Hugh DeSamper, Director of the Press Bureau of Colonial Williamsburg, at Williamsburg, Virginia, whose enthusiasm, knowledge of the subject, and friendly help did much to make this book not only authentic but great fun to do. They too are fine craftsmen in the art of helping an author with his research.

— C. B. COLBY

The Gunsmith

Gunsmithing was a skill which helped found, and later save, America. The colonists brought with them from Europe heavy, cumbersome weapons of uncertain accuracy. They were often as large as .75 caliber and required great lead balls as bullets, and a lot of powder to fire them. American ingenuity produced the marvelous Pennsylvania rifle, later to be known as the "Kentucky rifle" because of its use by many famous frontiersmen from that area. These rifles were long, often 6 feet in length, and fired a small ball of about .44 caliber. This saved lead and powder, both precious and hard to come by in the wilderness. The rifles fired a ball patched (wrapped) in a piece of thin leather or homespun cloth, greased to make ramming down the barrel easier. All work on these weapons was done by hand. Above (left), Master Gunsmith Wallace Gusler, of Colonial Williamsburg, bores a rifle barrel, using the same equipment as in colonial times. At right, above, he patiently shapes one of the full-length gunstocks for his exact replicas of the early weapons. On the opposite page is a general view of a typical gunsmith's shop where firearms of all kinds were designed, made and repaired. Within their range, these marvelous Pennsylvania shoulder arms were as accurate as the weapons of today, and their makers, the gunsmiths, among the finest of American craftsmen.

Boots and Saddles

The bootmaker and saddler did much to keep the early settler going, whether on foot, horseback, or on wheels behind a horse. Their skilled fingers made fine boots, shoes, belts, bullet and powder flasks, harnesses and saddles. Anything of leather, from trunks to trinkets, came from their cluttered shops. Above is a typical bootmaker's shop with the craftsman at work on a heavy soldier's boot. Note the many special tools on his bench and the wall behind. Many a bootmaker made his own tools. On the opposite page is a typical harnessmaker's shop. Note the wooden forms behind the craftsman. These were made to hold and display harness and saddles. The harnessmaker is working on a bridle with "winkers" or blinders (square portion just above his hands). These winkers prevented the horse from seeing to the side where sudden movements might frighten him. The long tongs by the bench were used to clamp leather together for heavy stitching. The bootmaker and harnessmaker were rightly admired and respected for their importance to colonial life.

The Tinsmith

The tinsmith was a skilled worker with sheet tin, solder, shears and punches. He made basins, tea canisters, toys, lanterns, snuffboxes, tinderboxes, candle molds, milk cans, foot warmers, and anything else which had to be made from lightweight metals. Many of his products were real works of art, such as the pierced tin lantern shown above. Although they are sometimes referred to as "Paul Revere" lanterns, these round pierced tin lanterns were quite different. The authentic Paul Revere lantern was square with four glass sides, not a bit like this round lantern with the conical top. The tinsmiths not only made and repaired all kinds of tinware but designed much of it themselves, for they were true artisans. This skilled craftsman at Old Sturbridge Village, Massachusetts, shows how the sheet tin was punched over a wooden block. A candle was set inside the lantern and its light shone through the punched-out holes. Tinsmiths used a wide variety of tools for folding, rolling, crimping and bending tin into many shapes as required. They could cut, twist and solder the thin metal into almost any shape for any purpose. Many of these wares were sold throughout the countryside by "tin peddlers" who carried their products in horsedrawn carts. Antique tinware is much in demand today.

The Broommaker

Although the humble product of this craftsman was usually relegated to the kitchen, its maker was in great demand. Every housewife had to have at least one broom. These were made from special "broom corn" raised just for this purpose. The tops of this corn were woven and lashed to a broom handle with heavy twine and then trimmed square across the sweeping end. The test of a well-made and trimmed broom-corn broom was whether it would stand erect on the trimmed ends. Once securely attached and bound to the broom handle, the heavy stub ends of the cornstalk, shown sticking out by the crafts-man's right hand, were neatly trimmed off close to the handle. Tension on the heavy binding twine was maintained by the foot treadle wheel. This skilled craftsman is shown at work in Old Sturbridge Village, Massachusetts.

9

The Cabinetmaker

The cabinetmaker was a highly skilled and valuable craftsman, for he not only made cabinets but all types of furniture as well. Above is a view of a typical cabinetmaker's shop of two hundred years ago. The craftsman at the right is polishing the pedestal of a small three-legged table or stand, while the two men in the background sharpen tools on a hand-turned grindstone. Note all the tools required for this exacting woodwork. On the opposite page (top) a master cabinetmaker puts the finishing touches on the pediment (top decoration) of a highboy, a high chest of several drawers mounted on decorated legs. Note the beautiful and intricate turning and carving. Lower photo shows an apprentice turning a huge wheel to spin the wood-turning lathe used by the cabinetmaker to turn round legs, arms and other turned wooden parts of his masterpieces. Long wooden objects on wall are clamps used to hold large wooden sections together for fitting and gluing. This completely furnished and working reproduction of a two-century-old cabinetmaker's shop is in operation at Williamsburg, Virginia.

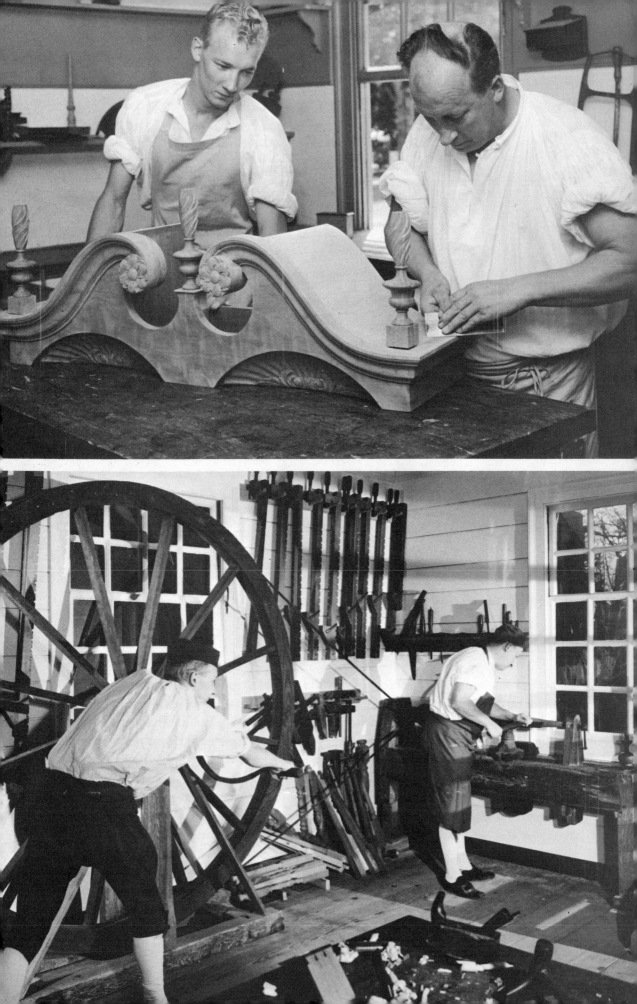

Shingle Making

The skill of the shingle maker was in constant demand, for, with the exception of a few thatched buildings and the rarer slate-shingled dwellings, all buildings of any size were shingled with wood. These handmade shingles were split from a quartered section of a log with a froe driven with blows from a maul or "beetle." Above, the craftsman is riving (splitting) a shingle from a log quarter. The froe, a one-handled metal blade, is held in his left hand while the maul is held in his right hand and pounded upon the top of the blade. The odd-looking device at the right is a "shingle horse," shown in use on the opposite page at the top. Foot pressure, as shown, holds the split shingle securely while it is trimmed into finished shape with a two-handled draw knife. Lower photo shows craftsman with an armful of finished shingles. Note broad-blade hatchet. Thomas Jefferson once wrote that "to rive and draw 500 shingles is a common day's work" and that "a man may join [lay] 3,000 shingles a day." This craftsman of Colonial Williamsburg demonstrates his skill in authentic costume of the period.

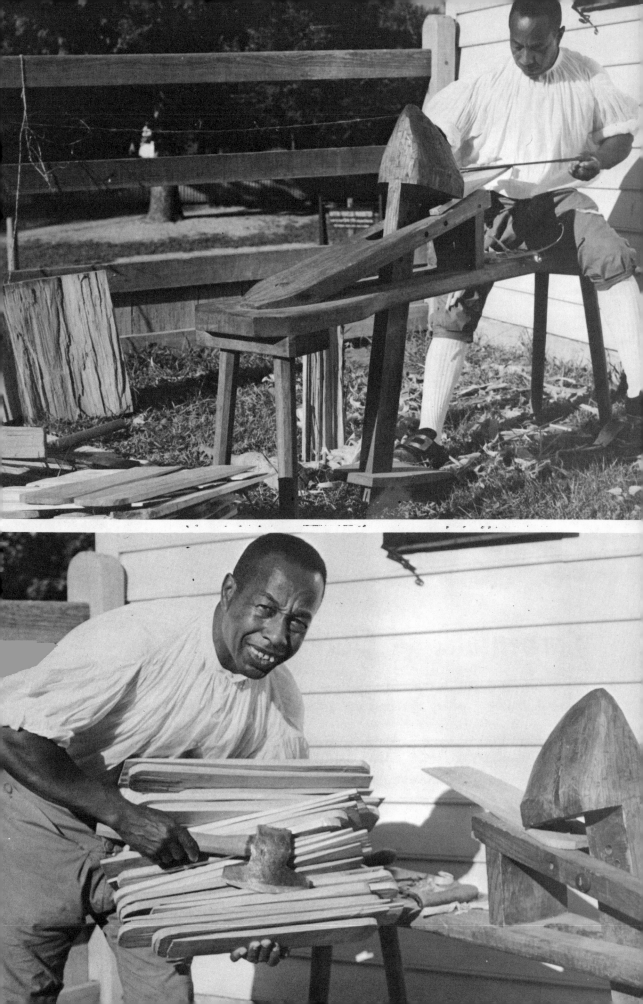

Carpenter and Clockmaker

Every colonist had to be a sort of jack-of-all-trades and through necessity many became skilled in a variety of simple yet exacting crafts. Toolmaking was an important one. Here a worker completes a wooden-toothed rake. The wooden teeth were hand-shaped and then driven through the crossbar of the rake with a wooden mallet. Note pitchforks against fence in the background. These were made from split poles or tree forks. The various old tools (auger, draw knife and mauls) shown on the workbench are all authentic for the period of two hundred years ago. Fences, ladders, stools, implements, as well as the tools used to make them, had to be designed and made by hand. In the early days of our great nation "handmade" meant skilled and careful workmanship, for, almost without exception, the craftsmen of the time took pride in their products and their skill in making them. On opposite page a skilled clock and watchmaker plies his trade. These experts also sometimes made jewelry and all kinds of delicate machinery and instruments, as well as many of their own tools.

The Blacksmith

One of the most important of all early American craftsmen was the blacksmith. He made all iron articles for the farm and home, from horseshoes, tools and candlesticks to cooking implements, shutter hinges, beautiful wrought-iron grills, gates and sign frames, and the all-important nails. It has been said that nails were so precious at times that when a house had burned the ruins were carefully picked over, not for valuables, but for the nails that might be salvaged. Above is an exact reproduction of a 200-year-old smithy shop showing a hooded forge with the big bellows mounted to the right, on a level with the fire. On the opposite page another type of forge is shown. In both types the huge bellows is operated by a hand lever. Note the various vises, anvils and tools used by the blacksmith, as well as the horseshoes on the overhead racks. The little four-legged "dog" in the forge (opposite page) holds tools and iron stock up out of the hot ashes and makes them easier to pick up. The fireplace above is in the restored area of Williamsburg, Virginia, and the one on the opposite page at Old Sturbridge Village, Massachusetts.

There were specialists among blacksmiths as well as in other crafts. Some turned their hands to making marine hardware such as boat fittings, harpoons, anchor fittings, metal parts for boats and tools used on shipboard. Others specialized in wrought-iron gates, fences, benches and sign frames. Above is master blacksmith John Allgood making a colonial sign frame for the historic area of Williamsburg, Virginia. He not only makes the beautifully twisted and curved metal pieces for the frame but designs them as well. Note the other sign across the walk. The bending and twisting of heated iron is a skill by itself. The blacksmith does this with hammer and muscle, using the horn of the anvil as shown on opposite page. Various shapes and sizes of tools are used for bending, twisting and cutting and the master craftsman in iron is expert in all these skills. The author's great-grandfather was a blacksmith and some of his handmade nails were used in construction of the author's present home.

The Silversmith

The silversmith had an important place in early American times, for he not only made fine jewelry but all kinds of utensils and silverware for table use. He made articles ranging from thimbles, buckles and snuffboxes to candlesticks, toothpick cases (then considered good taste) and silver spurs. He also made all kinds of dishes, teapots, soup ladles, sugar tongs, watch chains and cases, jewelry and trays. The photo above shows a Williamsburg silversmith hammering out a silver dish over an anvil or "stake" set into a tree stump. Rounded stakes such as you will note on the bench beyond and in the vise were also used for various types of wares. On the wall behind him you will note an assortment of still other stakes used for this shaping. On the opposite page another silversmith is polishing a vase or flagon with rottenstone (decomposed siliceous limestone). Many a silversmith called himself a "goldsmith," as it sounded better, but the vast majority of these craftsmen worked almost exclusively with silver.

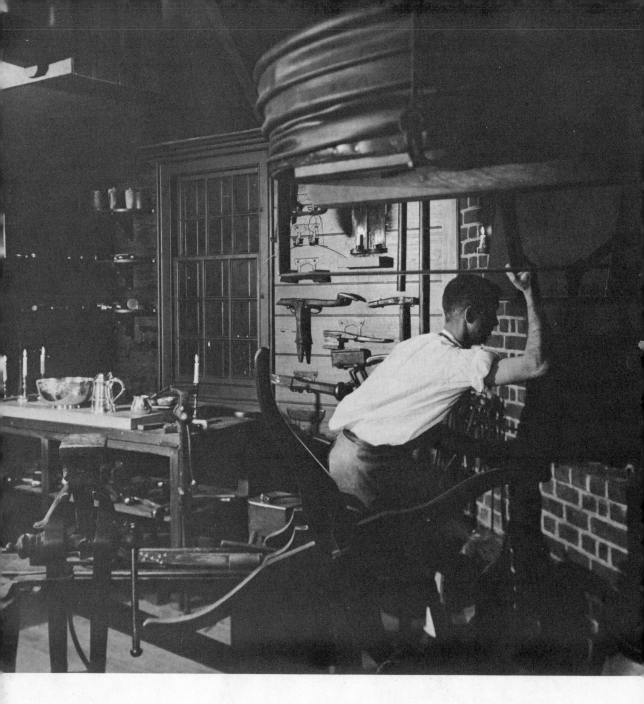

Many silversmiths smelted their own silver and used a forge in the formation of many of their beautiful products. One of the most delicate types of work was making fine silver or gold wire for bracelets and other jewelry, for inlaying in gun and pistol stocks and for decorating fine pieces of tableware. To do this, the metal was stretched to the proper size in the drawbench on the opposite page. The rod of silver was inserted in the clamp at the near end of the bench and the other end was gripped in the jaws of the unit on the end of the leather strip. By turning the windlass the silver was stretched into a thin wire of the right size for the intended use. By using different dies various sizes and shapes of wire could be made.

Pewter Caster or Pewterer

Those who could not afford silver utensils often used those made of pewter. Pewter was an alloy (mixture) of several metals, with tin as chief ingredient combined mainly with copper and antimony and small amounts of lead and other metals. The best pewter was only about 4 percent lead, as use of this metal cheapened the article, made it soft, and was also dangerous because it could cause lead poisoning. (Some unscrupulous pewterers, according to one pewterer I talked with, used to put as much as 25 percent lead in their wares.) A few pewterers traveled with a portable forge such as shown above. Some itinerant casters would give one pound weight in new pewter for three pounds of weight in old or broken pewter which they would remake into new. In the photo above the young pewterer is pouring molten pewter into a brass mold to form a pewter spoon. It cools in seconds and then is taken from the open mold, trimmed and polished. On opposite page at top you can see the same mold with the opening at the end of the bowl for pouring in the pewter. The mold comes apart in two halves for easy opening. Below this is shown a collection of roughcast spoons and sets of buttons similarly cast in a mold. These will have to be cut from the base bar and polished. Pewter was used for tankards, plates, platters and many other inexpensive utensils.

The Printer

The early printer sometimes made his own type. This might be made from either wood or metal. The type was set into a form, face up, and inked with leather pads as shown on the opposite page. Then a piece of paper was placed over it and the whole form run in under the printing press itself, as shown in photo above of another press of similar type and operation. Once the form was in place, a hand lever was pulled lowering the flat surface onto the paper and pressing it against the type below. When the press was released and raised, the printed form was moved from under it and the printed page removed. Note inking pads in racks in top of press frame. The type had to be set backwards, as in a rubber stamp. In the background of the photo opposite you can see a typesetter at work. Note another page already set into its form ready for later printing. Such printing was slow and the pressure of the press had to be just right or the page would be too dark or too light. These craftsmen developed great skill in setting type and printing all kinds of work, from handbills and newspapers to fine books.

The Bookbinder

The art of the bookbinder, as exemplified by these craftsmen, is almost a lost art today. Binding books in finely tooled and embossed leather requires great skill and patience. Above, a craftsman is stamping the leather cover with an embossing tool while the volume is held in a special vise. Beside this photo is a beautiful example of his fine craft. The binder makes a design and then stamps it in gold leaf with special tools right into the leather, a painstaking and slow process to assure perfect design and lasting beauty. On the opposite page a bookbinder is arranging and sewing the signatures (groups of folded pages) into a completed book ready for its cover. Today this is done by machine, but as with other early crafts, every bit of such delicate work was done by the skilled hands of expert craftsmen.

The Peruke Maker

The peruke maker, or wigmaker as he was perhaps more commonly known, catered to both the wealthy and middle classes, for a wig was considered an essential by many of all stations in life. There were many styles and purposes. In the photo above you will see several types popular a century or more ago. At the lower left, on a wig block is a "caul" made of ribbons and fine mesh into which the hairs were sewed. These cauls were made to the exact measurements of the customer's head (preferably shaved at the time) and determined whether the wig was to be a wig "with ears," that is, with the ears showing, a "half-ear" wig with ears partially covered or a "full-bottomed" wig with the ears completely covered. Once the skullcap or caul had been covered with hair, often helped out with some horsehair, it was set in whatever fashion the customer wished and then tinted with colored powders to the right shade. It was not unusual for a wig to have a slightly blue tint. On the opposite page a peruke maker combs out a simple wig. Note that it has the pigtail enclosed in a black silk bag. This style of wig was preferred when traveling, as it not only protected the pigtail, but the back of the collar from soiling.

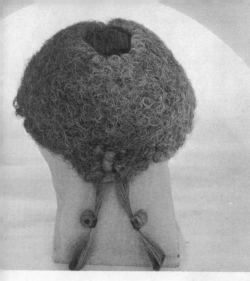

Above are two types of wigs. The upper one was known as a "legal wig" and was frequently worn by lawyers. The lower photo shows a handsome type of wig with twin pigtails, each tied with ribbon. These wig ribbons or bags were usually of black silk or taffeta. There are as many as 115 different types of wigs on record and about the only color they did not come in was red, which was termed a "disagreeable color" and almost never used. On the opposite page we see a gentleman having his wig powdered. The cone over his nose and face protected him from the fine powder. Often these powdering masks covered the entire face with holes cut for the eyes. In restored area of Williamsburg, Virginia, you can see a wigmaker at work in his well-furnished shop.

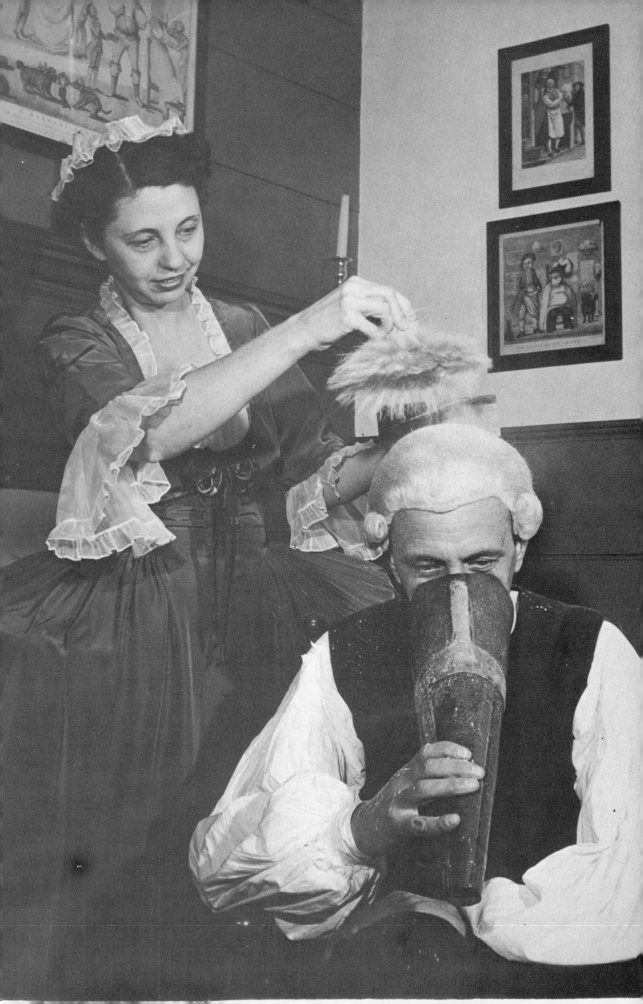

Candlemaking

Candles were the usual form of light in early America and their making was a continuous chore for someone in the household. They were made from tallow, bayberries, beeswax and spermaceti. The latter was a waxy solid separated from the oil of the sperm whale and the dolphin. Candles were made by dipping and molding. In the first process, wicks were tied to arms as shown in photo above, and then repeatedly dipped into molten wax. After each layer had hardened it was dipped again and again until the candle was of proper size. Photo on opposite page shows an expert candlemaker at the Colonial Williamsburg restoration, in Virginia, dipping groups of candles attached to a revolving rack. Each candle took as many as 25 to 30 dips before they were of usable size. After the layers have hardened, almost as soon as exposed to the air, they are redipped. After the final dip they are trimmed and cleaned for use.

In the photo above we see candles being made by the poured process. Wicks are run up through the metal molds and tied to an overhead stick. The molds are set into wooden racks and melted wax is poured into each candle mold to harden. When hard the individual molds are removed from the frame and dipped into hot water so that the candle will slip out of the metal form. Note candle coming out of mold held by woman. Note also the mold for making eight short candles on the table in background. On opposite page we see another candlemaker at Old Sturbridge Village, Massachusetts, using backs of two fine old chairs to hold her bayberry candles for drying. Note bunches of bayberries on mantle over fireplace. Lower photo shows a fine collection of old candle molds ranging from huge single candle molds to some holding as many as two dozen at a time. The fine art of candlemaking can still be seen at many historical restorations and is well worth watching.

Spinning and Weaving

Before the spinners and weavers can begin their work they must have the material with which to work. This was generally wool, cotton, or flax, from which linen is made. Wool is sheared from sheep, cotton is picked from bushes and flax is broken away from the hard inner stems of the plant by skilled flax breakers as shown above. This way of breaking the stiff wooden stems of the flax plant so that the outer fibers can be separated has changed little since Biblical times. Once the flax, cotton, or wool has been obtained and cleaned, it is carded (straightened and cleaned) and then spun into thread for the weaving. On the opposite page the woman is spinning the flax fibers on a small flax wheel. Fibers from the hank of flax above her left hand are fed together in one long continuous thread which is wound on the bobbin below her right hand. The thread's thickness is controlled by the amount of fibers fed into it by the spinner. The larger wheel in the background is a wool spinning wheel. Both are operated by the feet of the spinner.

Once the supply of thread is obtained, it must be woven into cloth. The finer the thread the finer the material produced on the loom. The loom shown above at left gives a good idea of their size and general appearance. Photo at right shows a close-up of the weaving itself. There are two sets of threads and between them the operator slides the shuttle filled with thread from side to side. When the shuttle (in the left hand here) has passed to the other side, the position of the two layers of threads in the loom are changed (lower changing places with upper) and the shuttle slid back again between them. The heavy bar hanging from above is pulled toward the operator after every change in thread position and trip of the shuttle, to force the threads close together for a tighter weave. This homespun material was frequently coarse and scratchy but the finest materials were often made on similar looms by skilled weavers capable of handling the thin threads from which delicate fabrics could be made. At many historical restorations spinning and weaving can be seen as carried on centuries ago.

The Shipsmith

Back in the days of "iron men and wooden ships," a particular kind of "blacksmith" was in great demand. This was the "shipsmith," skilled in the making of every type of ironwork for the shipbuilder, sailor, whaler or ship chandler. He knew all the tricks of making harpoons and lances (above) for the whalers, rail and bowsprit fittings as well as small hinges, hatch fasteners and a hundred other types of hardware used on ships. Note the bellows and hooded forge in the fine photo above from Mystic Seaport, Mystic, Connecticut, where the shipsmith can be seen at work. These experts with the forge, anvil and hammer were not only skilled ironworkers, they knew what the seafarer needed. Some of them had even gone to sea to learn firsthand the requirements of the mariner and his sailing ships. They had to know how to make and repair all kinds of marine hardware and often how to make the very tools they used in this exacting work, from the "bellows nails" used to hold the leather to the sides of the bellows, to iron cutters and tongs. The shipsmith was a true craftsman and proud of his profession and products.

41

The Sailmaker

Another early maritime craftsman was the sailmaker, specialist in canvas, cordage and use of the fid and palm and needles. Above is the sail loft at Mystic Seaport. The sails of early ships were made and repaired in lofts like this one. These lofts were enormous, for the sailmaker needed space to spread out the great sections of canvas from which the sails were made. Note that the stove to heat the loft was suspended on a hanging platform to keep the floor area uncluttered. On the opposite page (top) is a collection of sailmakers' tools. The long pointed implement at the top is a "fid," used to separate the strands of a line or rope for splicing. Just above the canvas toolbag are two "palms." The sailmaker wore one across his palm and used it to push the heavy needles through the tough material, much as a seamstress uses a thimble on her finger. Above these palms are awls for punching holes, and a needlecase. Below this collection of tools is a view of the mast hoop shop where the wooden hoops to hold the sails to the masts and spars are made. These come in various sizes to fit the different masts. If you visit a restored sailing vessel, look for these hoops about its masts.

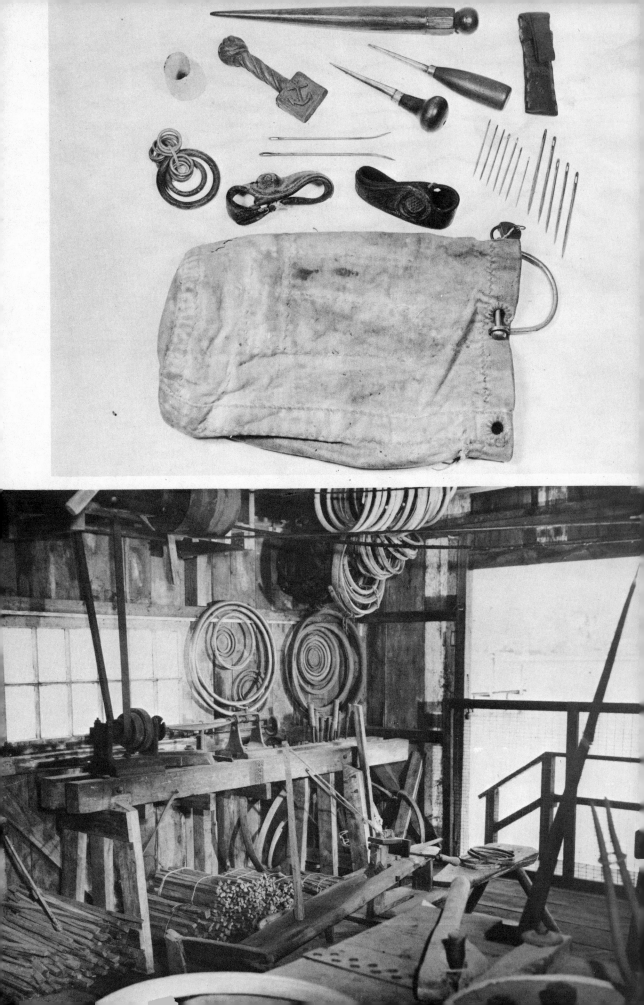

The Ropewalk

Every sailing ship required miles of cordage, from small hand lines to giant hawsers. These were made in a seaport or shipyard ropewalk, a long open building large enough for the machinery ropemaking demanded. At the top is shown the spinning wheel for making rope yarn from the hemp or sisal fibers. These fibers were hackled (combed) through the steel pointed hatchels shown on the floor, to straighten the fibers so they could be spun into rope yarn. At the top of the opposite page, bobbins of this yarn are mounted in a rack so that the yarn can be fed through holes arranged in concentric circles in a plate. Lower photo shows the traveling forming machine which pulls the yarn through the plate and twists it into a strand. Laying the strands into a rope is the last process of ropemaking. A laying machine, similar in appearance to the forming machine, twists these strands into the finished rope. Every size and strength of rope needed was produced by the skilled craftsmen of the ropewalk, who did much to keep the fleets of trade, military and whaling ships on the seven seas.

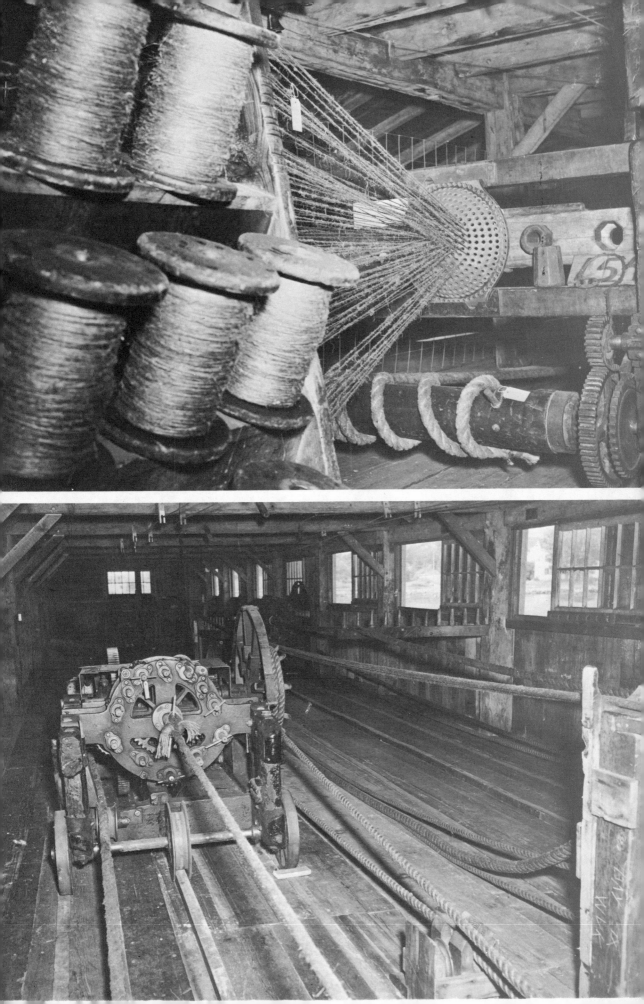

The Cooper

Before the age of metal and plastic containers, much of the world's goods were shipped, stored and protected in wooden kegs, casks, barrels and hogsheads. These were all made by the cooper, a craftsman with woodworking tools. The barrel staves were hand-shaped as shown in the photo above. The craftsman is hollowing out the inside of the stave held in a "horse" by pressure of his foot, which causes the upper arm of the horse to grip the stave. Once the stave has been shaped and the sides tapered to correct curve depending upon the size of the barrel, they are fitted into a form, as shown on the opposite page at the top. A rope and windlass is used to pull the tops of the staves together so a metal or wooden barrel hoop can be fitted down over the ends to hold them in place. Once held in place with sufficient hoops, a "croze" was used to cut a groove around the inside of the top of the barrel. Into this groove the barrel head was pounded to seal the end. Once in place, the barrel hoops were pounded down to tighten the grip of the grooved stave ends on the head by forcing them tighter together. A well-made and well-hooped barrel or cask was the perfect product of a skilled cooper.

The Wood-Carver or Ship Carver

To go to sea without a suitable figurehead set into the bow of the ship was almost unthinkable for the early mariner. Skilled wood-carvers designed and carved to order everything from grim admirals to well-upholstered ladies, and from eagles to flags and animals, to ornament the bows of all types of sailing vessels. Once carved, they were painted in bright colors and gold and silver. Some were rather crude while some were masterpieces of the wood-carver's art. Those craftsmen who specialized in figureheads for ships were known as ship carvers, although they often augmented their marine business by carving tavern and shop signs as well. This photo shows the wood-carver's shop at Mystic Seaport, Connecticut, where an expert craftsman still turns out masterpieces in wood. Photo, left, shows workbench of wood-carver and wall racks of many tools required in this craft. At right is a splendid example of a figurehead designed to go under bowsprit of a vessel.